A PROTESTANT PASTOR DISCOVERS MARY, MOTHER OF JESUS

Dr. Paul J. Young

MARY, MARY QUITE CONTRARY

Mary, Mary, Quite Contrary

A Protestant Pastor Discovers
Mary, Mother Of Jesus

Dr. Paul J. Young

© Copyright 2020 by Dr. Paul Joseph Young

No part of this book can be reproduced in any form apart from the consent of the author. Short parts may be used in a review.

Pictures in book are from free sources.

DRPAULYOUNG.COM

Dr. Paul J. Young was a Protestant pastor for 35 years and became a Catholic in 1999. You can see his bio on his website. He is the author of many books that you can find on DrPaulYoung.com

Based on old poem:
"Mary, Mary, quite contrary"
BY MOTHER GOOSE

Mary, Mary, quite contrary
How does your garden grow?
With silver bells and cockleshells
And pretty maids all in a row.

Like many nursery rhymes, it has acquired various historical explanations. One theory is that it is religious allegory of Catholicism, with Mary being Mary, the mother of Jesus, bells representing the sanctus bells, the cockleshells the badges of the pilgrims to the shrine of Saint James in Spain (Santiago de Compostela) and pretty maids are nuns.

Wikipedia

1

Wanting To See The Real Man, Not His Mother

YEARS AGO I STEPPED INTO THE HOME OF ERNIE HARWELL, hall of fame announcer for the Detroit Tigers. As I walked into his home, he introduced me to his mother and then left to make a call.

I sat there for a moment, making small talk, all the while thinking that I had come to see Ernie, not his mother.

Then it occurred to me that if I wanted to know Ernie better, I needed to take advantage of this time with his mother. So I began to ask her questions about her son and what he was like growing up. In the space of nearly ten minutes, I gleaned some valuable insight to this friend of mine, information that made me appreciate him even more.

At the time I was a Protestant Evangelical pastor with a driving focus in my life - getting to know Jesus and helping others do the same.

Thirty years later, God clearly indicated that I should become a Catholic. There was, however, a major problem, Jesus' mother. I wanted my focus to be on Jesus and not clouded by those who surrounded him, including his mother.

I believed she was a good, even a great person. But that was about it. I wanted to spend time with Jesus, my friend and master, not with his mother.

2

To Know the Real Man Better, I Needed To Know His Mother

YET THE MORE I BEGAN TO LOOK AT MARY and pay attention to her, the more I liked this unusual woman.

I discovered that she was always putting the focus on Jesus. In fact, that was her purpose in life, to point people to her son. After all, didn't Mary know Jesus better than any other person?

She helped him take his first steps, knew where he was ticklish, what his favorite foods were, and that he always got up early to pray, prayers that sometimes she could hear, their intimacy, openness and power.

Mary also saw her son's love for the Hebrew Scriptures which he memorized as an early child. She observed his complete obedience to his heavenly father.

Yet in all of this, Mary never bragged about the intimate details of her son like other women did as they boasted about their children's accomplishments. There was no, "My Son's on the Honor Roll," plastered on the back of her cart. Nor did she write an op-ed piece for the Jerusalem Times, talking about all his miracles and how great "MY." son is.

She was amazingly quiet. It was never about her parenting skills and all she did. It was instead all about her Son, Jesus. He was her focus, her life.

3

Now I Can Get To Know Jesus Better

BEFORE BECOMING CATHOLIC, LIKE MARY, JESUS WAS MY FOCUS TOO. And now, I find that spending time with Mary pays off with big dividends. She always does what she does best, help me to more fully understand her son.

Thank you, my dear Mother,

for always pointing me to Jesus.

I was the one that was contrary,

not you.

4

Questions about Mary Mother of Jesus Christ

THERE ARE MANY QUESTIONS ABOUT MARY that come to mind. Thousands of books have been written that seek to help us understand this great woman and her place in God's plan to bring us redemption.

I will only cover some of these questions. If you want more insight, look at the books I recommend later.

(1)

DID MARY HAVE OTHER CHILDREN besides Jesus? The Bible talks about Jesus' brothers and sisters. Doesn't this counter the teaching of the Catholic Church?

The Catholic Church as well as some other well known Protestants teach that Mary was ALWAYS a virgin as well as some well known Protestants.

Note these statements from famous Protestant leaders.

Martin Luther, the main leader of the Protestant Reformation, wrote:

> *When Matthew says that Joseph did not know Mary carnally until she had brought forth her son, it does not follow that he knew her subsequently; on the contrary, it means that he never did know her.*

> *Christ, our Savior, was the real and natural fruit of Mary's virginal womb. This was without the cooperation of a man, and she remained a virgin after that. Christ was the only Son of Mary, and* **the Virgin Mary bore no children besides Him**. *I am inclined to agree with those who declare that 'brothers' really mean 'cousins' here, for Holy Writ and*

the Jews always call cousins brothers. (Sermons on John)

Zwingli, an early Protestant leader wrote:

I firmly believe that Mary, according to the words of the gospel as a pure Virgin brought forth for us the Son of God in childbirth and **after childbirth forever remained a pure, intact Virgin**. (Zwingli Opera, Corpus Reformatorum, Berlin, 1905, v. 1, p. 424)

Even **John Wesley**, founder of the Methodists wrote in 1749:

I believe that He [Jesus] was made man, joining the human nature with the divine in one person; being conceived by the singular operation of the Holy Ghost, and born of the blessed Virgin Mary, who, as well after as before she brought Him forth, **continued a**

pure and unspotted virgin. (a letter written to the Roman Catholic Church)

(2)

WHY PRAY TO MARY since there is "Only one mediator between God and man, the man Christ Jesus," as stated by St. Paul to Timothy?

It is true that Jesus Christ paid for our sins and in this way is our own personal Savior and redeemer. Mary is not a redeemer in the same way Christ is. Yet she can intercede and mediate for us in her own unique way.

Even as I ask someone to pray for me, to intercede and mediate (as a priest does - for we are all made priests in Christ), so too I can ask Mary to intercede and mediate for me. This in no way takes away from the redemptive and salvific redemptive action on Christ's part. It is he who shed his blood for the redemption of all humankind.

It is interesting, as we look deeper into this question, that Catholics and Protestants approach prayer differently.

Catholics see all those in the family of God, whether those who have gone on to eternal life or those still alive on the earth as a GREAT AND GRAND GROUP as a whole, all working together to bring about the Kingdom of God.

ALL of them are engaged in this activity.

So, as a Catholic prays to Jesus, he also asks the whole company of saints to pray with him, including the Holy Mother of God, Mary.

Other Christians tend to ignore this great company, this great army fighting to bring in the kingdom of God. Why exclude them? Why not allow them to fight for you and to pray with you?

(3)

DO CATHOLICS WORSHIP MARY?

Absolutely not! We worship only the Father, Son and the Holy Spirit. Mary is not part of the Trinity! To think so is heresy. Yet we do hold her in high honor even as we do some of the greats of history like George Washington, Abraham Lincoln as well as St. Mother Teresa and so many others.

Mary, the Blessed Mother of Jesus Christ, can even be held in a higher honor only because of her special favor, to be the vessel that gave birth to the King of the Universe, God in the flesh! What honor! Therefore it is right and good that we should honor her too in a very special way.

(4)

How can Mary hear all our prayers since millions are praying to her at the same time?

Do you understand time? If a million people wanted to speak to you, you would have to take TIME to hear each one. And if you gave each of them a minute of your time, it would take a million minutes to hear each one, which is nearly 17,000 hours or approximately two years!

BUT THERE IS NO TIME IN HEAVEN. When you move into that spiritual universe, many of the limits we have here are removed. Thus what is impossible here is possible there so that Mary can hear us all, even when millions pray through her to Jesus.

(5)

IT SAYS IN THE BIBLE THAT "ALL HAVE SINNED and come short of God's glory." How is it then that Mary is said to not have sinned? Isn't this a direct contradiction of the Scriptures? Doesn't Mary call God her Savior?

It is true that Mary needed a Savior. This is why she calls God her Savior. Yet you need to understand what she means.

Our Holy Mother was SAVED from original sin BY GOD'S GRACE. On her own, Mary would have been a sinner just like you and me. But, because of God's special plan to make her into a perfect vessel for his Son, Jesus Christ, he stepped in and did something unique, he SAVED HER from sin by preventing her from any participation in it.

And even as the man Jesus was protected from sin through the working of the Holy Spirit, so too, Mary was saved from sin, and by the power of the Holy Spirit lived a perfect life.

Yes, all have sinned except for Jesus and Mary, Jesus because he is the Holy Son of God and Mary, because she was to be the holy vessel for the incarnation PROTECTED BY GOD'S GRACE.

5

Protestant Ignorance

IT IS A SHAME THAT TOO MANY PROTESTANT PASTORS and leaders have very little understanding of Marian doctrines and dogmas.

I know.

I was very ignorant, even though I had a ThM from Dallas Theological Seminary and a Doctorate from Biola University's Talbot School of Theology. This ignorance showed through my use of Scripture in a way that demonstrated a lack of study and understanding of any part of Marian Doctrine and Dogma.

I was taught nothing about Mary in seminary, and a great seminary at that. All their focus was on Jesus and neglected to say anything of importance about his Blessed Mother.

So I gave simple Biblical answers that were void of any deep and respectful thought, and thus undermined the truth and our Saviors' Mother.

What a shame for me to neglect her!

How could I have ignored the woman God chose to bring Jesus into the world?

Martin Luther didn't, as well as some other early Protestant leaders. But today, glib answers are given that show a total lack of study and understanding of the truth, both Biblical and what was believed by the early Church.

Don't fall for it until you have done your own research. And read broadly.

You must ultimately answer why the earlier Church had far more respect and devotion to Mary than most Protestants today.

You see, Jesus told his Apostles and their successors that The Holy Spirit will guide them into all truth. This is why many truths we believe as Christians are not found in the Bible.

The Trinity is not mentioned. Jesus being both perfect humanity and absolute deity is not clearly taught in the Bible. It took the Church hundreds of years to conclude who Jesus was - guided by the Holy Spirit.

Much of the Church at that time did not believe that Jesus was God, and they used the Bible to prove their stand. Yet, the Holy Spirit kept working on the Apostolic team (the Bishops) to where they finally caved into the truth - not clearly taught in Scripture.

So too with Mary. We have very little in the Scriptures except that she was FULL OF GRACE (no room for sin) and the powerful woman promised by God who would, through her seed, bash the head of Satan and reign as Queen of the heavens (see Gen. 3, Rev. 12).

So we must listen to what the Holy Spirit revealed to Church leaders. The Bible is great but not sufficient to reveal all of the truth. We need the Church, headed up by Christ and managed by the Pope and other Bishops, who, when they speak in unison, declare teaching from the mouth of the Holy Spirit. It is NEVER their teaching but that ONLY GIVEN BY THE HOLY SPIRIT.

This is where the TRUTH comes from. Our Holy Bible came from THE CHURCH, and by the Holy Spirit guides us into the truth.

It was St. John Henry Newman who said:

To be deep in history is to cease to be Protestant.

When we cease to be ignorant of Church history, we will stop believing the Protestant distortions about Mary.

There are too many educated pastors and leaders who are ignorant of Church history and what the early Church taught and practiced. Don't be one of them. Free yourself from pastors and leaders who distort the truth.

The Holy Spirit will guide you.

6

The "Hail Mary" Is Biblical

So often it is declared that the Rosary and the Hail Mary are not Biblical.

Really?

Most of the "Hail Mary" comes right out of the Bible. You can see it clearly in Luke 1.

And the part that doesn't, comes from a strong Biblical Tradition of the early Church.

How absurd for some to say the Hail Mary is not Scriptural.
Open your Bible and see for yourself.

And...why not repeat the words of the angel and Elizabeth? They are words filled with great content, mystery and doctrine. Say them. Meditate on them. Allow this great mystery to impact your soul.

The angel said:

Hail Mary Full of grace,
the LORD is with thee

Elizabeth, Mary's cousin, said:

Blessed are you among women, and
Blessed is the fruit of your
womb (Jesus).

The 4th century, Mary was declared

to be the **Mother of God** at a Church Council - Council of Ephesus.

Holy Mary, Mother of God,
pray for us sinners
now, and
at the hour of our death.

Amen

7

Depth In Our Prayer Life

Saint Dominic was encouraged by our Blessed Mother to bring about changes in his society by praying THROUGH Mary to Jesus. The power that came through these prayers was not just the focus on our Blessed Mother, Mary, but also on the Mysteries that were the focus of each day, Mysteries that would teach those who meditated on them the content of their Faith.

In one sense, all one needs to know about their Christian faith is the whole of the Rosary - the Apostles creed and the Mysteries.

To meditate on these, to plunder the depth of them is to enter into the rich heritage of our faith, taking us deep into the person of Mary and Jesus, into the throne room of God where our prayers are being heard.

IT IS A POWERFUL ACTION THAT WE ARE DOING!

It must be noted too that we should not just say the Rosary but PRAY the Rosary.

Prayer is not a one sided talk with God. It should be a dialogue where we speak and allow time for listening. There are many who say the Rosary, recite it each day in a rote way and are done with it.

Though this is not bad in itself, we all can say the Rosary more powerfully and intentionally for our families and friends. As we do so, we are grabbing the attention of Mary and the powerful assistance of Jesus Christ our Lord. We enter the Holy of Holies and are communing with them.

Let's do our best not to rush through these holy moments. And instead of SAYING the Rosary, PRAY it, our hearts open to meditation and contemplation as we spend time in the presence of Jesus and his Blessed Mother, Mary.

Pope Paul VI clearly points out the right way to pray the Rosary when he says:

> *Without contemplation, the Rosary is a body without a soul, and its recitation runs the risk of becoming a mechanical repetition of formulas in violation of the admonition of Christ, 'In praying do not heap up empty phrases as the Gentiles do; for they think they will be heard for their many words.'*
>
> Matthew 6:7

He goes on to say that:

> *We should make every effort to meditate on the Mysteries each and every time we pray the Rosary. The Rosary is no substitute for Lectio Divina (a prayerful reading of Scripture); on the contrary, it presupposes and promotes it.*

As you pray the Rosary, be open to God's voice as you talk with him. He wants to carry on a conversation with you. And he will do this as you pray the Rosary for yourself, each family member or friend. He will stop you, at times, make you slow down and help you to pray specific, powerful requests as you intercede for a family member or friend.

This means REAL PRAYER will be happening - not just you doing all the talking. You will be dialoguing with God as you pray through the Rosary.

A Decision To Make

YOU NOW HAVE A DECISION TO MAKE. Will you spend some time researching the ROSARY and our Blessed Mother, Mary? Open yourself to the HISTORICAL truth of Jesus' mother - the one who birthed Jesus, the man, and Jesus, God of all time, holy, infinite and full of absolute love.

Go ahead. Search. DON'T LET FEAR KEEP YOU FROM FULLY BELIEVING in a mother who is **YOUR MOTHER** - made your mother at the cross when Jesus gave her as a mother to John, a sign of giving him as mother to the whole Church of which you are a part.

Go ahead. Prayerfully make Mary you Mother. It will open a whole new dimension to your Faith and a whole new way of communing with Jesus.

Let his mother plead for you to her Son. Don't be contrary to her desire to surround you with her love, holiness and passion and make sure you make it to heaven to live with her, her Son, the Holy Spirit, God the Father and all the saints…FOREVER.

Go ahead and find your real Mother for the first time!

IF YOU HAVE QUESTIONS About The Catholic View And Practice of Praying To Mary And Her Role In Heaven, Read These Good Books.

1. **Refuting The Attack On Mary** by Father Mateo

2. **Behold Your Mother** - a Biblical and Historical Defense by Tim Staples (A Protestant Convert)

Let me know if you have any questions: Go to my website <u>DrPaulYoung.com</u> and look up how to contact me. I would love to dialogue with you.

My Prayer For You

May you discover the value
Of having a heavenly mother
Who will help you better
Understand her Son,
Jesus Christ.

May your Blessed Mother
Take your prayers
And in love
Bring them before her powerful Son
Who listens to her
Because of her maternal care
And grants her requests.
With joy.

Amen

FREE BOOKS
FOR
YOU!

Be sure and go to DrPaulYoung.com and sign up for a **free book**, a book designed to take you to a new level in your walk with God.

And keep watching this site because new free books will be offered periodically.

Last, **pray for our ministry**. We are seeking to change the hearts and souls of thousands of people around the world and need your prayers. Send me a note at pauljyoung@mac.com if you will for this us.

Thanks, and God bless you!

Be sure and look at Dr. Paul J. Young's books on the Rosary:

How To Pray The Rosary For Your Family - Change your family through prayer. This is a powerful way to see your family impacted by your prayers. These prayers will make a great difference now…and forever.

I'm Praying The Rosary For YOU! - You can impact a family member or friend by sending them this book. It has many places where you write their name showing that you do, in fact, pray for them in specific and powerful ways. It is a life changer!

The PERSONALIZED Rosary - Try praying this personalized Rosary for 30 days and see a tremendous difference in your life. The joy it will bring and the peace will be beyond words.

Dr. Young also wrote a novel that's a thriller entitled,

Once Divided
*Passion and Romance
in a Battle for Religious Unity*

It's the story of a Protestant Pastor who became Catholic - through much tribulation. It will also give you insight into our Blessed Mother, Mary.

Many of my books are only $2.99.

What a deal!

Dr. Paul J. Young

Education:

University of California, Fresno, B.A in English

Dallas Theological Seminary, Th.M (Masters in Theology)

Biola University, Doctorate of Ministry with emphasis on pastoral psychology (working with Talbot School of Theology, Rosemead School of Psychology and other schools)

Dr. Paul Joseph Young

Dr. Young helped grow one of the largest churches in the Dallas/Ft. Worth area as its pastor, working with thousands of people, developing his skills both as a minister, communicator and a counselor, working with hundreds of people and developing his unique therapy techniques.

For seven years he was C.E.O. of Community Bible Study International, working in over 60 countries of the world, sharing his message of hope and joy. He held seminars on anxiety, anxiety, stress, fear, anger, and a host of other topics, seeking to bring healing to the thousands in need.

Dr. Paul's communication skills has made him a favorite speaker around the world. He lives with his wife and best friend, Diane. They have five children and 14 grandchildren.

More than anything, Dr. Paul lives to help people find the joyful, peaceful life they deserve.

This is a

DrPaulYoung.com.

Publication

_____

You can get any of my books at
DrPaulYoung.com

Check them out.
There are over
50 books
to choose from,
from psychology
to theology
and even a fast passed novel - a real
Catholic thriller!